How to Start a Tattoo Shop

Start a Successful Tattoo Shop on a Budget!

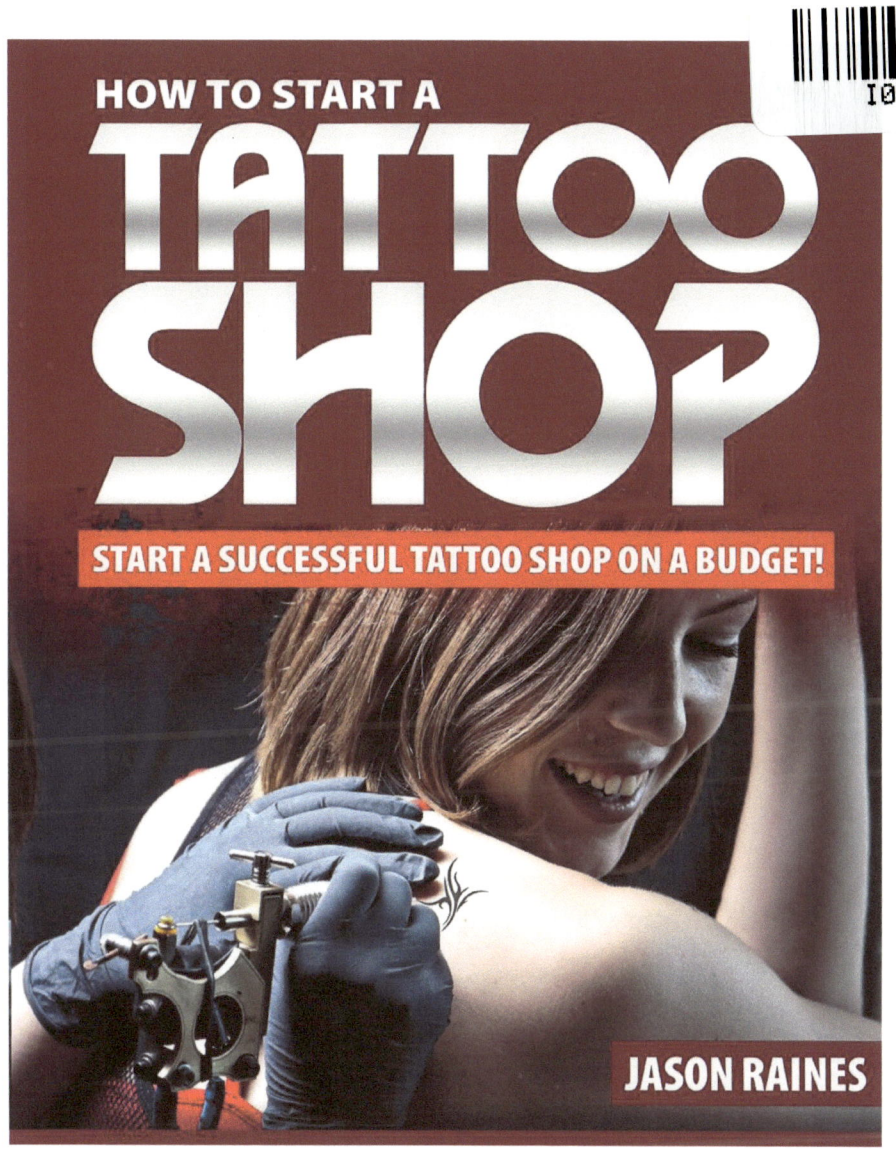

Copyright © 2014 How to Start a Tattoo Shop by Jason Raines

How to Start a Tattoo Shop

Table of Contents

Overview

Chapter 1 Laws   4

Chapter 2 Equipment   5

Chapter 3 Costs   9

Chapter 4 Location   10

Chapter 5 Advertising   11

Chapter 6 Business plan   12

Chapter 7 Business license   13

Chapter 8 Health permit   13

Chapter 9 Tattoo supplies   14

Chapter 10 Office furniture   15

Chapter 11 Qualified staff   17

Chapter 12 Sterilization   18

Chapter 13 Tattoo Machines   20

More tattoo info available at: http://dragontattoosupplies.com/

Overview:

Tattooing has become extremely popular these days and it still continues to grow each day. Many people these days get tattoos, doctors, lawyers and even many older people. The massive tattoo industry has no sign of slowing down anytime soon. This is the reason why many feel getting into the tattoo industry is the best thing ever. Owning a tattoo shop can be extremely lucrative for anyone.

Many tattoo shops can make up to six figures a year or even more. You don't even have to be a tattoo artist to open a shop but with a good business mindset you should be able to do well in this industry. The best way is to actually have some tattoo training prior to trying to open the shop. It would be much easier to open the shop if you have some knowledge of the tattoo industry.

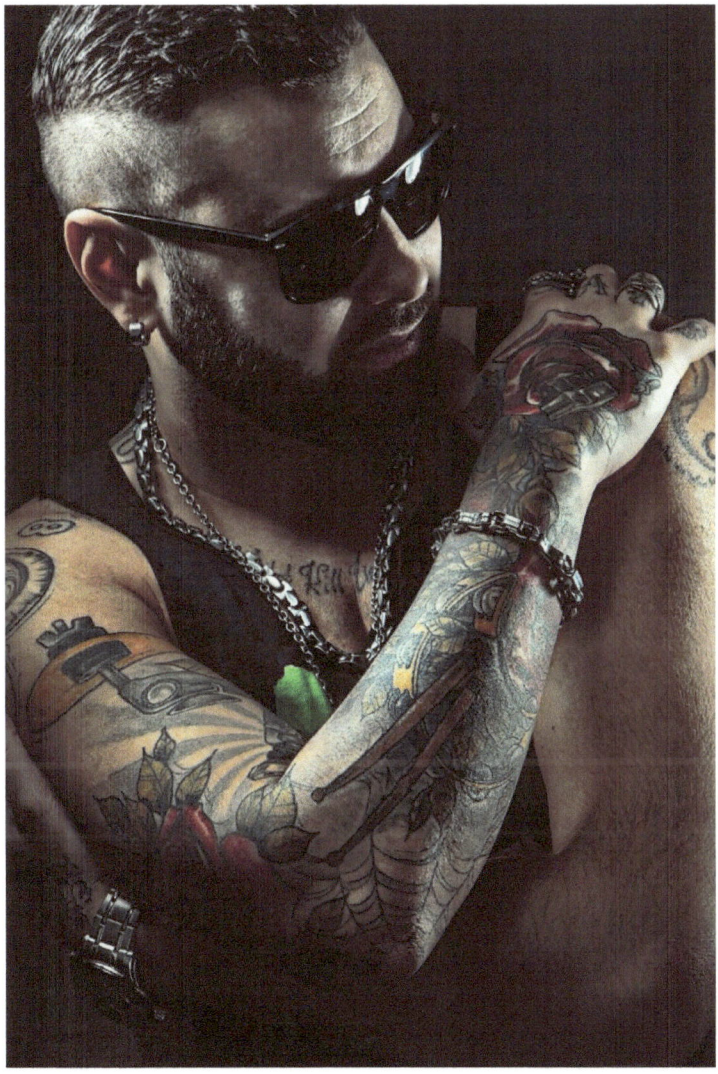

If you want to be in the tattoo business it can be quite the experience, a good experience and sometimes just down right crazy. Tattoo shops are not like many other businesses, you never know what can happen over the course of a day. People will come in and get the wildest of tattoos which can be really comical.

Women everywhere and people coming in trying to barter gadgets for tattoo work. People will try to trade all kinds of things for a tattoo. Making sure you are professional as possible. While this may sometimes be fun, wading through all this will lead to a successful shop and one that's talked about in high regards in their community. You want to have a respectable shop, not some place that people are scared to go to.

Chapter 1: Local laws

Contact your local health, city, state or county department to find out about tattoo business regulations in your area. The laws regarding tattooing and sanitation vary considerably across the country, but no matter where you live certain rules, regulations and limitations will exist. Many counties are different and have different laws concerning tattooing, what I find best to do is actually Google "local tattoo laws" for whatever city and state you're in. And you can actually print those out for your viewing and reference.

Some counties can be extremely sensitive about tattooing; in some states can be very flexible. Tattooing laws are extremely important information to find out before trying opening your tattoo shop. Some counties may even want you to have a licensed physician on staff, which by itself can run you an extra $40,000 a year for just a part-time physician. And that's on the low end. Now this is sometimes rare but it can happen, that's why it's important to check the local laws first.

 So make sure you thoroughly check your local laws or even head down to health department and talk to someone on staff. These laws will also impact how soon you open. Many counties require things that will need to setup a dispensary where you will need to clean sterilize and store your tools. This is usually is a separate area setup like a small kitchen, with a sink and cleaning area and sterilization area. You can also setup cabinets or an area to store your tools after sterilization.

 I mention dispensary because it's important to look at the area you want to open and make sure you will be able to make a dispensary, you will need to check and make sure that there will be plumbing available for the sink and everything that will be needed in this room. A proper dispensary will cost some time and money to build. Roughly 1k-5k for a nice one, these areas are important to have if the law permits it our not.

Tools in the dispensary will include:

Sink

Autoclave

Ultrasonic cleaner- to breakup ink in and on the tubes before final cleaning and sterilization

Sterilization pouches, various sizes

Tube cleaners-to clean the hard to reach areas, inside of the tattoo tubes

Alconox- ultrasonic solution

Sterilizer solution

Distilled water-for sterilizer

Spore test-to test if autoclave is working

Spore test log

Chapter 2

Section 1: Tattoo equipment

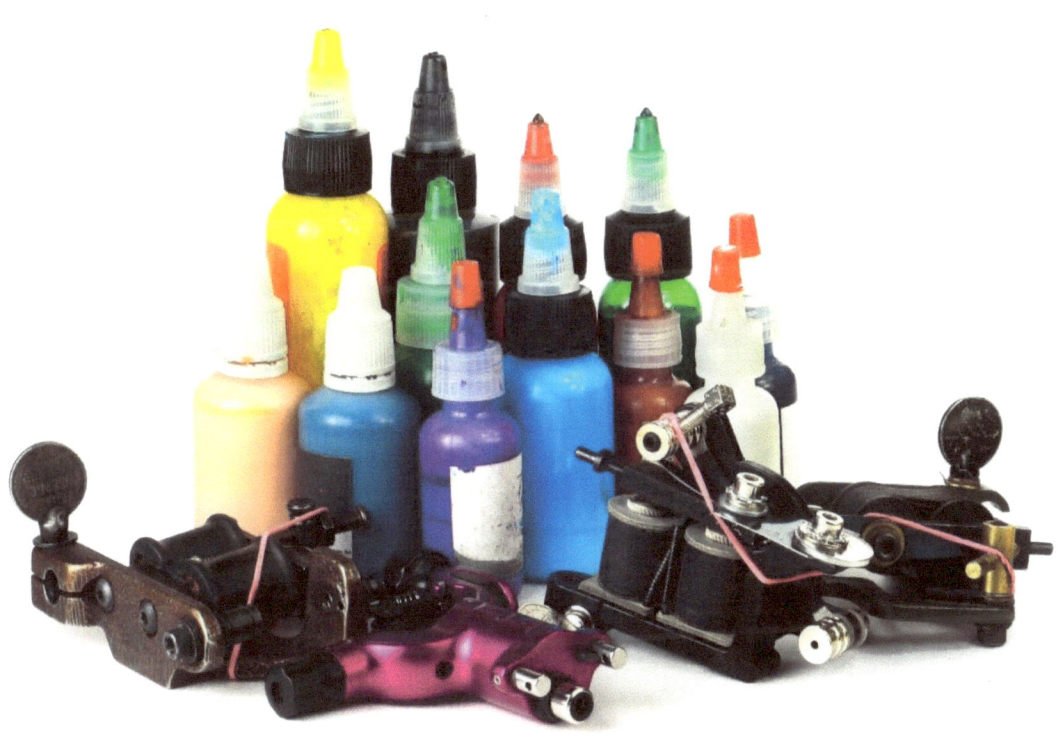

There is a lot of equipment in tattoo shops from your tattoo machines to artwork. We will go over each on this list.

Tattoo Machines- Quality tattoo machines will cost anywhere from $100-$500 for top quality hand built machines

Tattoo Ink - Quality tattoo ink will cost anywhere from $100 to $300 for a good set of tattoo ink

Power supply - You will only need a small, basic power supply to get started. You get what you pay for. I've been using a Dermagraphics power supply for 15 years with no problem. It costed $150 almost 15 years ago.

Foot Pedal and Clip Cord - Used to power the tattoo machine from the power supply

Needles and Tubes - All are single-use, disposable

Needles:

3 Round Liners

5 Round Liners

5 Magnum Shaders

7 Magnum Shaders

Make sure to get pre-made, pre-sterilized on the bar needles 25 of each should keep you busy for a while

Tubes:

4-8 Round Tubes (5/8")

4-5 Flat Tubes (1")

6-7 Flat Tubes (1")

For the liners I prefer a 5-8 diameter tube it's big enough for me not to get a cramp and small enough to get good control. Make sure you get 1 inch diameter for the shaders so it's comfortable to hold for long periods of time.

Rubber Nipples - typically 100 packs

Inks - Don't go cheap here, you get what you pay for. Moms, Starbrite and Millennium color all perform well. Kuri-sumi for black and gray wash

Ink Caps - Size #9 and #12 ink caps

Transfer paper - 8.5 x 11 transfer paper for making tattoo stencils.

Sharps container - For tattoo needle disposal

Supplies you can purchase locally:

Powder free latex gloves from Costco

A&D ointment or Vaseline 16oz jar

Two spray bottles

Rubber bands

Plastic wrap

Sandwich bags non zipper

Madicide

Scissors

Scotch tape

Rubbing alcohol

Dial liquid soap large refill bottle

Paper or Styrofoam cups

Bleach (for area cleanup)

Paper towels softer the better for wiping.

Rolling chair or stool with adjustable height

Massage table with vinyl non-porous work top that can be easily cleaned.

Chair with vinyl arm rest for client to be worked on.

Optional items:

Roll around storage cart with drawers for keeping supplies in one place.

Rolling salon station with table top and drawers let you move your work station with you to the client.

Dry lock pads for bandages and work area.

Plastic cord cover

Section 2: Shop equipment

Work areas will include several reclining chairs --- similar to dentist's chairs --- tables, lighted tracing tables, supply carts and large sized mirrors. The reception areas need a counter or desk, chairs, couches shelves to display "Flash" --- basic art designs --- and display cases if you are offering body jewelry. The office area generally requires a desk, chair and file cabinets.

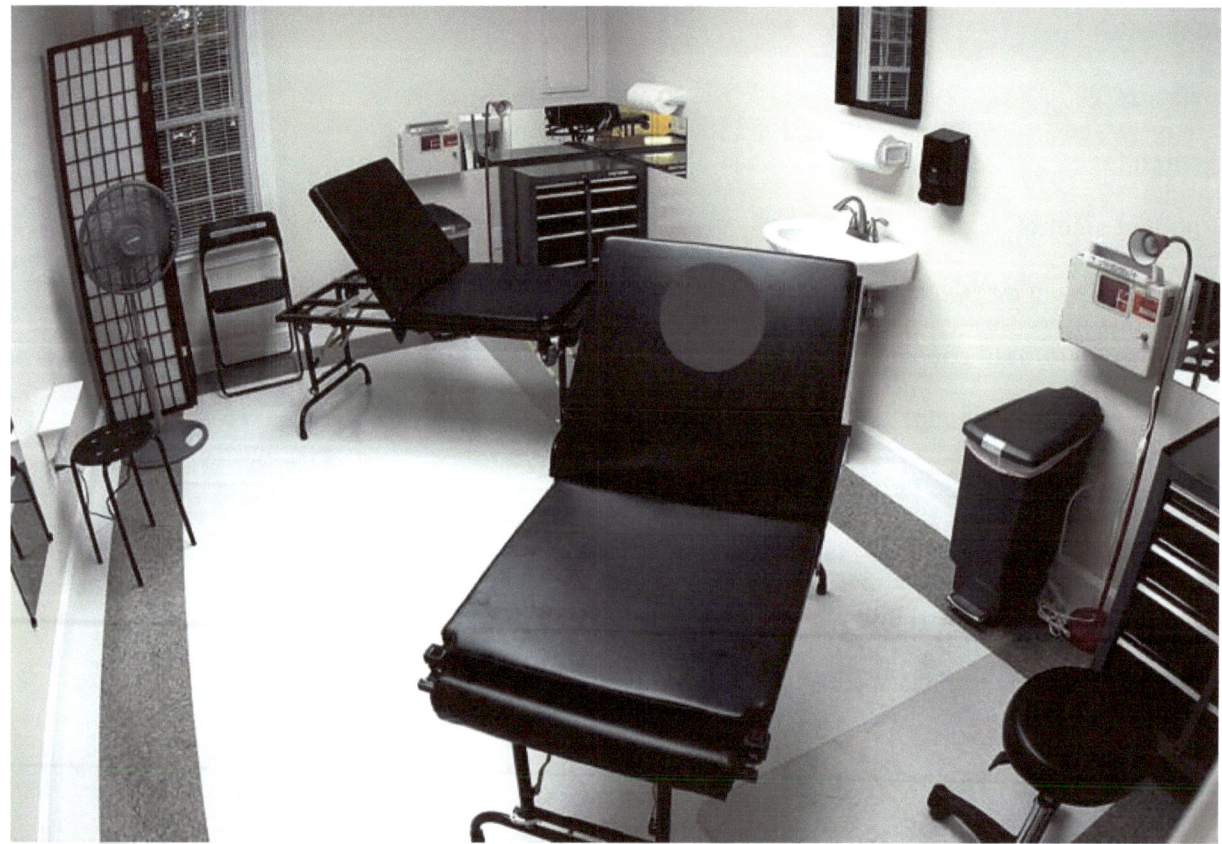

"Flash" Tattoo Designs-Flash designs are standard tattoos designs, purchased by a tattoo studio, for use in tattooing. The designs can be of various qualities. At best, some flash is quite attractive, while other flash designs are simplistic, or, at worst, awkwardly drawn and distasteful. Many shops have a section for tribal, lower back tattoos, small quick tattoos and so on. That will help later when you're directing clients to a tattoo that will fit them.

Chapter 3: Costs

You'll notice that tattoo supplies and equipment will be most of the investment. To open the shop you're looking at needing at least $10,000 on the low and $50,000 for a nice shop. After buying equipment supplies and everything else.

Buy and install all necessary furnishings to accommodate your artists and clients. Work areas will include several reclining chairs — similar to dentist's chairs — tables, lighted tracing tables, supply carts and large sized mirrors. The reception areas need a counter or desk, chairs, couches shelves to display "Flash" --- basic art designs --- and display cases if you are offering body jewelry. The office area generally requires a desk, chair and file cabinets.

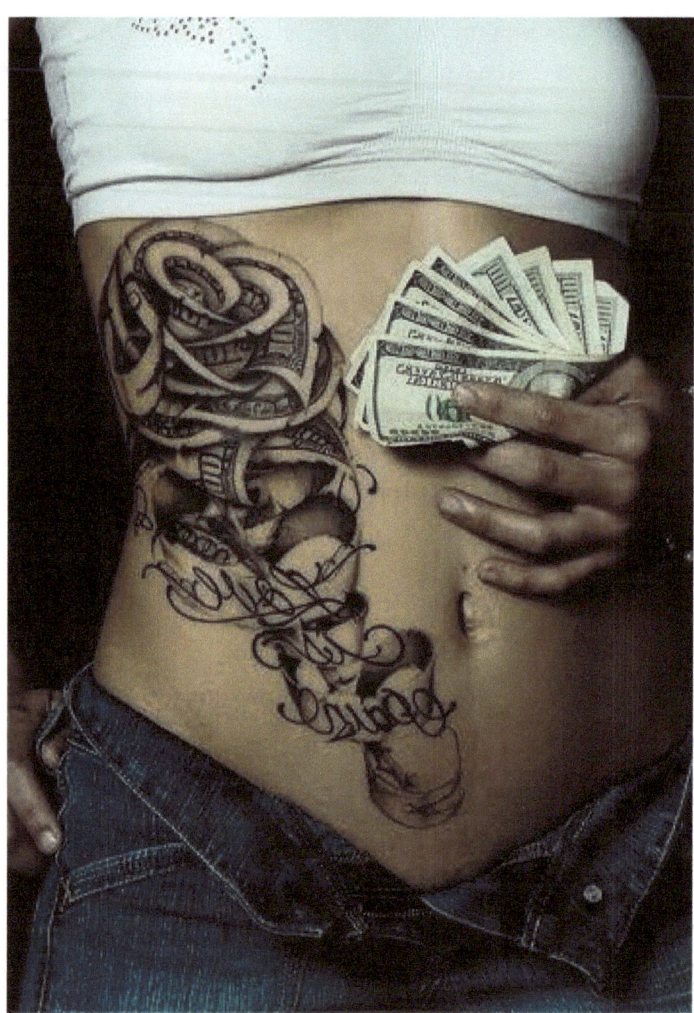

You will also need shop insurance for your tattoo shop. This can be really expensive in some areas. Here in California, it's around 2 million worth of insurance is needed and you usually, and you will have to put down $200-500 to start the policy and then you pay a monthly fee. Usually around 50 per month. That is best discussed with your insurance agent.

Leasing a location can be expensive, your dealing with commercial real estate and prices in small cities can be anywhere from $500-100 for a nice location. In bigger city's it will be more like $900-1500. And premium locations like Los Angeles where I live expect to pay 2000-1000+ very very fast! Its best to try to start small, then once you start making money you can upgrade to a better place or even a second location which is most profitable.

Chapter 4: Location

As with any business location is everything, you want to make sure you find a place where people can see you. Also this makes it much easier to get business when you have a location that can be seen from the road. Another thing to consider is the population of the area, if there's not a lot of actual people in the town it may be a bad idea to open up there, you're going to need to make sure you're going to have enough people to tattoo. If you want to have a lot of business.

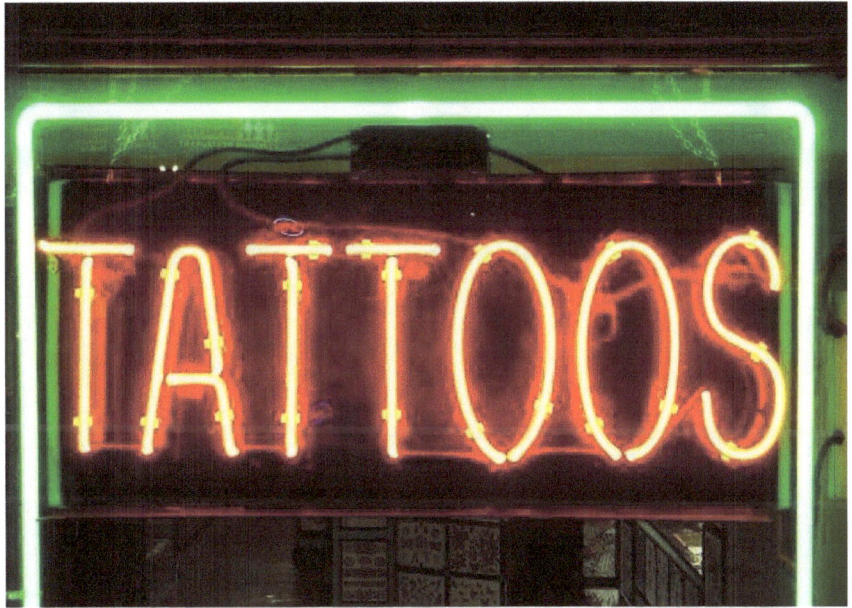

A lot of shops open near college campuses or in downtown areas where there are a lot of people including college kids and walk by traffic; this makes it a lot easier to get customers without having to do a lot of advertising. The less money you spend on advertising the more money you can put into your shop or other things or back into your pocket. The thing about shops with walk by traffic is you can just stand out front and get customers. Like hooking fish! Flyers work, road signs, sign holders, neon's are awesome. Signage is important for advertising and so people can see the tattoo shop from the street.

Chapter 5: Advertising

Advertising your tattoo shop is extremely important. And there's 1 million ways to do it, first thing you want to make sure you have the quality business cards for your business. This will represent your tattoo shop so we want to make sure they're nice with all your contact information on them legibly and even some pictures of your work.

Nice thick glossy cards can run anywhere from $100 to $200 for good quality cards, the better card the better it represents your business. Flyers are also good and can be handed out for quick business. There also good because you can fit a lot of tattoo pictures on them. Make sure that your work is clean and big enough to see and make sure your contact information is there with a website link. Even add your social media links and encourage clients to like or follow the shop.

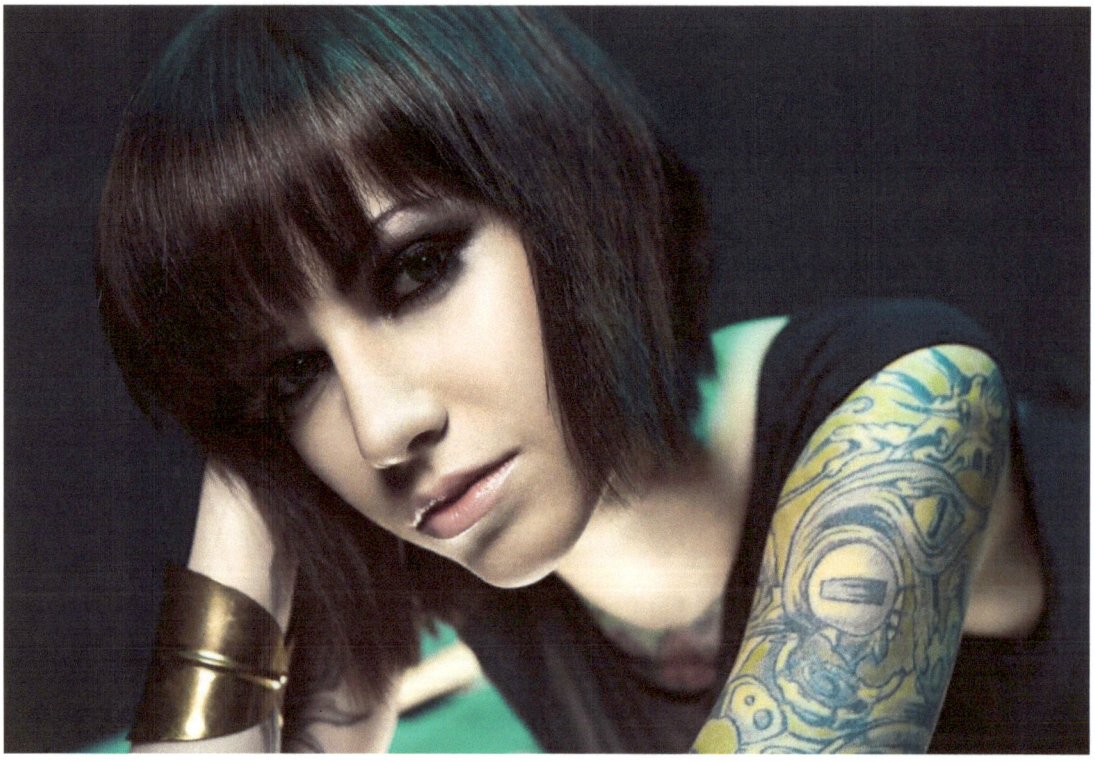

A website is also very important to your tattoo shop a shop without a website these days are definitely behind times. Even a basic website will be better than having no website at all. Many people when looking for tattoo artist these days usually use Google or other search engines online to find the tattoo shops locally. This will definitely increase the chances for you being found for people looking for tattoos In your area. Another thing is the good old Yellow Pages, not many people look there anymore but it can still definitely bring you extra traffic.

Yellow Pages are now online so make sure you sign up there. And also have to mention using Google places. This is very powerful for your business and costs nothing to setup or maintain. Local newspapers are also good for getting traffic locally. Just make sure you do a test at first before you sign any contracts. Many magazines will make you sign a six month to a year contract without even showing you any results, this is the last thing you want to do, at all costs.

Chapter 6: Business Plan

If you're looking for outside funding (say, from a bank), then a business plan may be a necessity. Even if it isn't, though, any new business owner should consider creating one before opening the doors. Creating a business plan forces you to consider aspects of the business that may have never occurred to you otherwise, and being prepared for them puts you at an incredible advantage down the road.

Chapter 7: Business license

Who needs a license?

Every shop or mobile unit that provides tattooing, body art, or body piercing must have a license.

Requirements

To get a shop, mobile unit, or event license, your business must:

- Have an outside entrance separate from any rooms used for sleeping or residential purposes.
- Have adequate toilet facilities for the use of customers located in or adjacent to the shop or business.
- Not use any room, except toilet facilities, for both residential and business purposes.
- Meet the zoning requirements of the county, city, or town where the business is located.
- Provide for safe storage and labeling of all equipment and substances.
- Meet local and state fire codes.

- Have at least $100,000 in public liability insurance for combined bodily injury and property damage.
- Be registered with the Department of Revenue.

Chapter 8: Permits

There are a few different permits and you'll need to open your tattoo shop.

Health department permit. Confirms your tattoo shop is up to standards of professional tattoo shop.

Zoning permit

Occupancy permit

Business license

Bloodborne pathogens certificate

First aid training and certificate

Chapter 9: Tattoo supplies

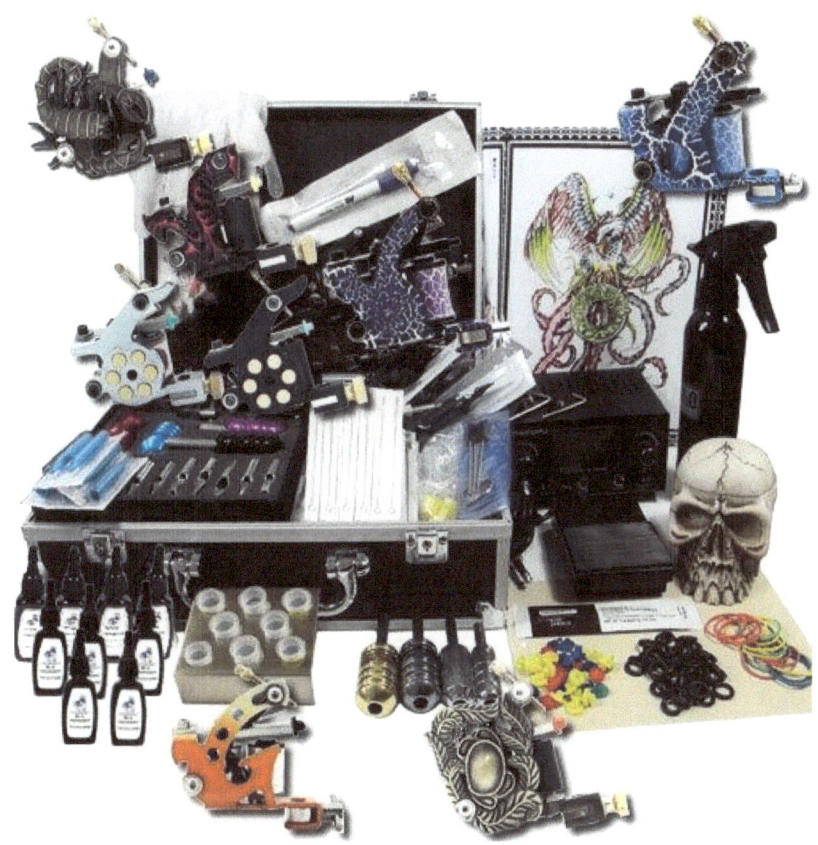

Its best to find a few different tattoo supplies that stock everything you need, you will become familiar with them, and it will be very easy to place your orders when you need. There are many well-known reputable tattoo supplies companies that have been in business for a long time and are most trusted. Here is a list of some:

1. Superior

2. National

3. Element

4. Dragon Tattoo Supplies

5. Kingpin

6. Worldwide

7. Cam tattoo supply

8. Eikon

9. Intenze

10. Lucky tattoo

11. Spaulding

12. Pulse

13. Time machine

Chapter 10: Office furniture

The office area generally requires a desk, chair and file cabinets. a computer to help keep track of appointments and shop inventory and revenue is important.

Some of the other equipment will be:

Thermal Copier- An important item that needs to be included in a list of tattoo supplies is a thermal copier. This piece of equipment allows the tattoo artist to make a copy of a design that can then be transferred onto the skin of the person getting the tattoo, making sure that the tattooed gets exactly what he or she wants.

TATSOUL sells many different tattoo chairs and chairs for clients, all of its high end equipment and can range in price form a few hundred into the thousands for their high end equipment, its defiantly worth it. copiers printers, tons of print paper and thermal paper. You don't want to run out of these things on a busy day.

Tattoo Shop Furniture and Equipment

Tattoo Work Table- This consists of a linoleum or glass top table to hold all of your tattoo supplies or equipment while you tattoo.

Tattoo Artist Chair

Choose a comfortable chair that you can sit in for long periods of time.

Customer Chair

A comfortable chair for customers.

A massage table, versatile, perfect for hard to reach areas.

This is used for customers who are going to be getting tattoos on their back or legs.

Light Source (adjustable)

This is a free standing adjustable light source you can use at various angles.

Paper Towels

Dispenser and Trash Can-Paper towels are used for all types of purposes while tattooing.

Chapter 11: Staff

Hire professional tattooists to sufficiently staff your studio. Depending on how big your shop is and how much clientele you expect to generate, you'll probably need at least one or two professionally trained tattooists. Before your grand opening, evaluate your potential amount of clients and be prepared by hiring a sufficient amount of professionally trained tattoo artists.

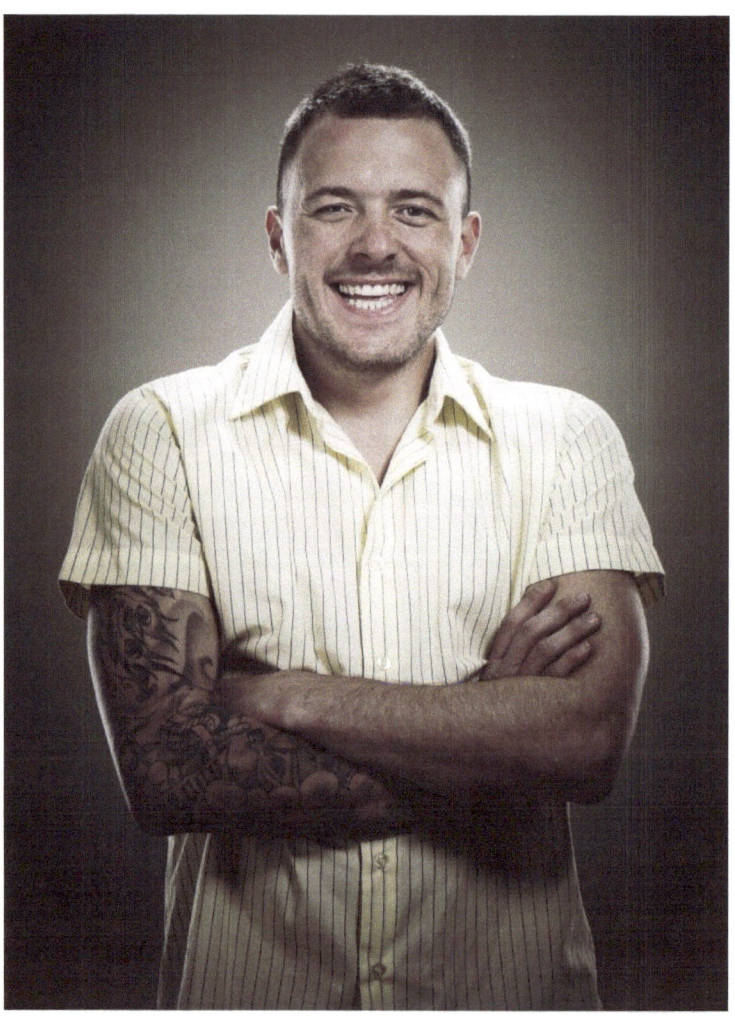

Another tip for hiring, many tattoo shops don't think like some of the big businesses. But if you take some of these tips and apply you it works well. I make an area on the website for artists to post there resume or signup for a job, and I collect and store this info, this way whenever I need a new artist I have a database of qualified artists to choose from.

Its best to adjust staff to shop policies as fast as possible, you should have written rules to give them and also at least biweekly meetings to discuss the rules and reiterate the rules. For a smooth running shop, and also go over shop news and info. Setting up a good structure and work environment is extremely important.

Chapter 12: Sterilization

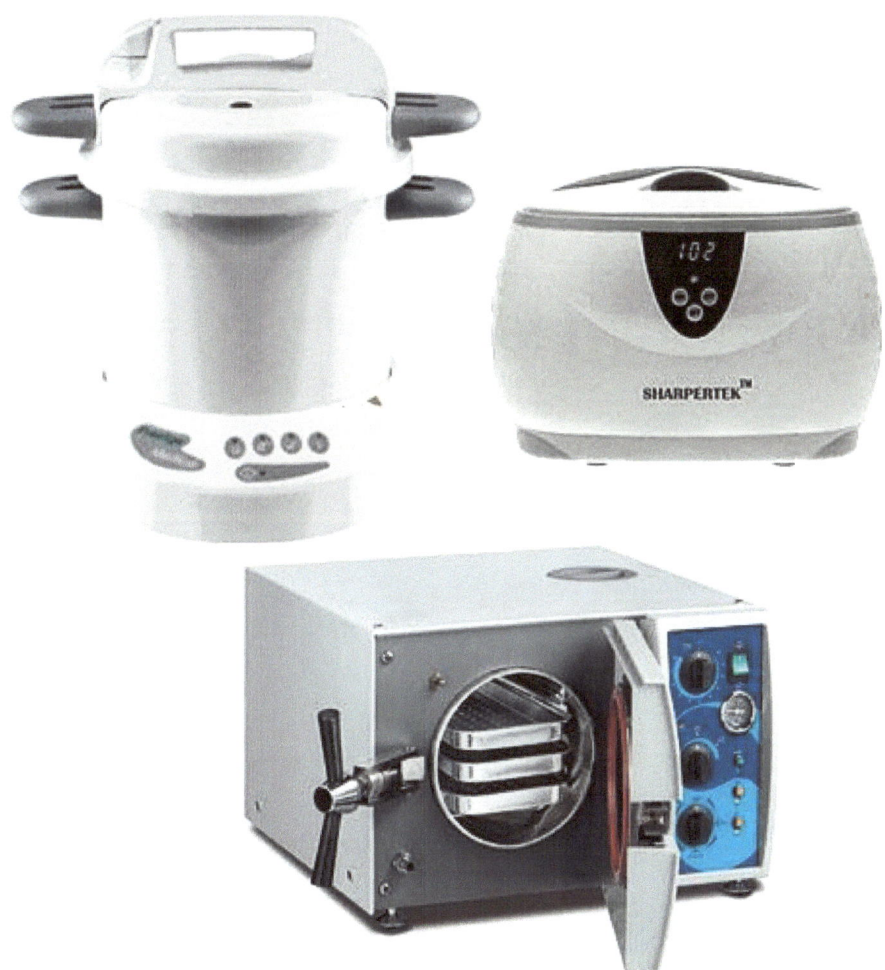

Sterilization Equipment List:

Autoclave (Stericlave)- used to sterilize the tattoo equipment.

Autoclave bags- where you put the tools after cleaning, then seal these bags and put them in the sterilizer.

Main Ultrasonic Cleaner and Solution- used to break up ink on your equipment before sterilization

Tattoo Machine Rack- Simple rack to hold unused machines.

Germicidal Solution- keeps sterile equipment clean.

Medical Equipment

Needle Trays- These are stainless steel trays that will hold your tattoo equipment

Various Spray Bottles- will hold a mix of your green soap solution and water

Small Glass Jar- This will contain sterile ink caps.

Stainless Trays- for your equipment.

Vaseline (Carbolated) - Used for stencils and skin.

Various Antibiotic Ointments and Solutions- These are used to wipe down the skin for healing.

Green Soap- This is used for cleanup and preparation. Please note that this soap is NOT used for sterilization purposes.

Disposable Razors- Used for skin preparation. It's hard to do a tattoo on a hairy mess on the body. ALWAYS use a fresh razor for each customer.

Various Handi Wrap, Bandages, and Hospital Tape-Used- For safely covering tattoos.

Rubbing Alcohol and Pads- Used for disinfectant on cleanups. Please note that this is NOT used for sterilization purposes. Use to clean the skin before tattooing.

Tongue Depressors- Used for the application of various ointments.

Stainless steel SHARP hospital scissors.

Latex Gloves- These are surgical latex gloves to be used when tattooing. You should NEVER perform any tattooing without the use of latex gloves. You are protecting yourself and you are protecting your customer. Make sure to check with your customer to make sure they are not allergic to latex. You can also have nitrile gloves when available.

Chapter 13: Tattoo Machines

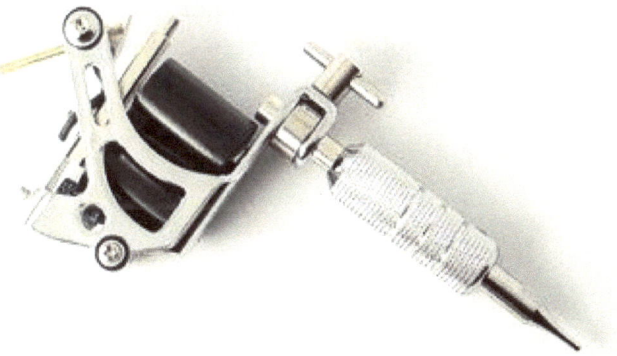

All tattoo machines basically work by driving the needle in an up and down motion to slightly open the first layers of skin just enough so the ink can be driven into the skin. It is the job of the tattoo artist to steer the machine in an outline or a pre-drawn design to complete the tattoo. Now that you have an idea of how the tattoo machine works it's time to get started using it. It is extremely important to learn how to use the tattoo machine properly if you eventually want to become a great tattoo artist. As I said previously, the machine doesn't do the hard work; that's the job of the artist.

The Five Basic Things You Must Remember about Using your Tattoo Machine

1) Proper angle – You need to be at a 45-degree angle in order to place the ink under the skin.

2.) Proper needle depth – Too much depth, and you are going to cause pain to your subject, and there may be unnecessary bleeding. Too shallow and the ink won't stay

3.) Proper machine set up – This is going to eliminate many problems for you. Practice setting up and taking down your tattoo machine. do this often in your first year

4.) Proper palm placement – Use your palm effectively to control and balance the tattoo machine.

5.) Last but not least. Practice, practice, practice

Make sure you have your business name and health department licensing setup before contacting tattoo suppliers they will require you provide your license information before you order. It's also important to pick a nice professional name for your tattoo shop.

If you have questions about anything please share them on our Facebook Page:

https://www.facebook.com/TattooTrainingGuide

For quality tattoo supplies and other tattoo training material released monthly visit.

Dragon Tattoo Supplies

http://dragontattoosupplies.com/

www.ingramcontent.com/pod-product-compliance
Lightning Source LLC
Chambersburg PA
CBHW050437180526
45150CB00006B/2571